The Bill of Rights

Seventh Amendment: The Right to a Trial by Jury

by Rich Smith

Series Consultant: Scott Harr, J.D. Criminal Justice
Department Chair, Concordia University St. Paul

VISIT US AT
WWW.ABDOPUBLISHING.COM

Published by ABDO Publishing Company, 8000 West 78th Street, Suite 310, Edina, MN 55439.

Printed in the United States.

Editor: John Hamilton
Graphic Design: Sue Hamilton
Cover Design: Neil Klinepier
Cover Illustration: Getty Images
Interior Photos and Illustrations: p 1 Constitution & flag, iStockphoto; p 5 student, iStockphoto; pp 6-7 Civil Courthouse, Getty Images; pp 8-9 multi-cultural jury, Getty Images; p 11 Wal-Mart class action suit, AP Images; p 13 No Trespassing sign, iStockphoto; p 15 Attorney addresses jury, Corbis; p 17 jury box, iStockphoto; p 19 truck driver, iStockphoto; p 21 woman signing contract, iStockphoto; p 23 Ketchikan's bridge to nowhere, AP Images; pp 24-25 police carry confiscated computer equipment, AP Images; p 26 U.S. Capitol, iStockphoto; p 27 unsigned contract, iStockphoto; pp 28-29 Attorney addresses jury, Corbis; p 32 U.S. Supreme Court building, iStockphoto.

Library of Congress Cataloging-in-Publication Data

Smith, Rich, 1954-
Seventh Amendment : the right to a trial by jury / Rich Smith.
p. cm. -- (The Bill of Rights)
Includes index.
ISBN 978-1-59928-919-9
1. Jury--United States--Juvenile literature. 2. United States. Constitution. 7th Amendment--Juvenile literature. I. Title.

KF8972.Z9S65 2008
347.73'052--dc22

2007014577

CONTENTS

Introduction

Santa Cruz County is a great place to live and go to school. It's located along Monterey Bay on the pleasant Pacific coast of northern California. More than 255,000 people call it home. Many residents came from Mexico and other countries of Latin America, and for these people Spanish is the language they prefer to speak.

Enrolled in the schools of Santa Cruz County are approximately 10,000 students who mainly speak Spanish. That can be a problem when it comes to taking tests written in English, which make little sense to students who are more comfortable speaking Spanish. And test questions that can't be understood are questions the test-taker almost surely won't be able to answer correctly.

In 2001, the federal government passed a law called the No Child Left Behind Act. This law required schools to do a better job of teaching their students. The law also required that students be given tests every so often to prove that they were getting a better education. But after a few years of taking No Child Left Behind tests, people in Santa Cruz County noticed that the Spanish-speaking students were not scoring as well as the law required. One reason was that those tests were written in English.

This was a problem for the county because the No Child Left Behind law punished schools whose students tested poorly. The schools of Santa Cruz County tried very hard to help the Spanish-speaking students achieve higher scores. But nothing seemed to work well enough to make the federal government happy. People in eight of the county's school districts got together and filed a lawsuit demanding that students be allowed to take tests with questions written in Spanish instead of English.

What does any of this have to do with the Seventh Amendment to the Constitution of the United States? Plenty. The Seventh Amendment guarantees the American people their right to take individuals, groups, and even entire governments to court when a wrong has been committed. But even more importantly, the Seventh Amendment guarantees the right to have such lawsuits heard by a jury.

Above: When the No Child Left Behind Act caused many non-English-speaking students to test poorly, people in Santa Cruz County, California, were able to file a lawsuit against the government thanks to the Seventh Amendment.

Here is what the Seventh Amendment says: "In Suits at common law, where the value in controversy shall exceed twenty dollars, the right of trial by jury shall be preserved, and no fact tried by a jury, shall be otherwise re-examined in any Court of the United States, than according to the rules of the common law."

Jury Duty

There is another amendment besides the Seventh that also mentions juries. It is the Sixth Amendment. However, the juries it talks about are those used in courtroom trials of people accused of criminal acts, such as murder, kidnapping, or theft. An act is considered criminal if it causes harm to the government or to society.

On the other hand, the Seventh Amendment talks about juries used in courtroom trials to settle disputes brought by a person, a business, or an organization against another (or even against the government itself). These are called *civil* cases, which usually involve anything that isn't a criminal act. For example, a person might take a business owner to court if the business owner is paid to provide a service and then never does. Or a business owner might take a person to court if the person receives a service and then never pays for it. It's called being sued when you're taken to court to settle a dispute. If you are the one doing the suing, you are the *plaintiff*, or *petitioner*. If you are the one being sued, you are the *defendant,* or *respondent*.

Civil cases don't always involve disputes over money. But in every instance, the person who goes to court wants to win. It doesn't matter whether the person is the plaintiff or the defendant. If you go to court, you want to win. And that is why the Seventh Amendment's guarantee of a right to a civil trial in front of a jury is so important.

Above: A woman walks into a civil courthouse in New Orleans, Louisiana. The Seventh Amendment of the United States Constitution talks about juries being used in courtroom trials to settle disagreements between people, businesses, or organizations. These are called civil cases.

A jury is a group of ordinary people from all walks of life who make decisions based on evidence presented to them. A judge also makes decisions based on evidence. But a judge is one person, while a jury is many. Also, a judge is expected to keep his personal feelings out of the trial, but a jury is allowed to let feelings help shape its decisions. The authors of the Seventh Amendment knew that it would be best to have juries decide civil cases because verdicts given by a jury would be more democratic. And being more democratic, those decisions would be easier for everybody to accept.

The Seventh Amendment says very little about civil court juries other than plaintiffs and defendants having a right to one. It says nothing about who can serve on a jury or how such juries are to be selected. Those details were left to Congress, the courts, and state legislatures to work out. However, most everyone agrees that civil court juries should be like the criminal court juries described in the Sixth Amendment. What the Sixth Amendment says about juries is that they must be impartial. Impartial used to mean the jury could not be made up of people who would benefit in some way from how the trial turned out. For example, a jury would not be impartial if one of the jurors were married to someone who is an employee of the business being sued. Today, impartial still means juries must have no personal stake in the verdict. But it now also means that juries must not reach verdicts based on the popularity or unpopularity of the plaintiff or the defendant.

It once was thought that juries made up of fewer than 12 people were too small to be impartial. Twelve was believed to be just the right number for a proper balance of different viewpoints. Having such a balance of viewpoints would help the jury make truly reasoned discussions about the evidence and then reach a verdict everyone could trust. That's why juries in the United States at first always had 12 members. Later, the federal Supreme Court decided that a jury with less than 12 could be just as fair and effective. The High Court then set the smallest legal size for a jury at six people.

Above: It is believed that the best jury is one made up of people from all walks of life.

Class Action Lawsuits

EVERY SO OFTEN you'll learn in the news about someone filing a *class action lawsuit*. The word *class* in this situation does not have anything to do with schoolrooms and students. Here *class* means a number of people grouped together by something they all have in common. In a class action lawsuit, what they have in common is that they all have suffered harm at the hands of the same person or thing.

A class action lawsuit is a way for those many harmed people to all sue at once. Otherwise, they would each have to file their own individual lawsuits against the person or thing responsible for causing harm. That might not be too big a problem if, for example, five different people were suing. Having five separate lawsuits would not slow the wheels of justice too much. True, the same witnesses would have to be called five different times, and the same evidence examined on five separate occasions. But the court system could probably handle that. Where the wheels of justice surely would come to a screeching halt is if the number of people wanting to file a lawsuit against the same defendant were not five but 500, or 5,000 or 50,000.

With a class action, all those victims' lawsuits are combined into one single court case. It's very efficient and doesn't clog up the court system. If the victims win, they all share in the victory. If the court awards money to make up for the harm they suffered, then they all share in the big payout.

Some defendants also like the idea of a class action. They much prefer defending themselves against one lawsuit instead of many. It's easier to do, and it's also better in the event they lose. In a class action, they stand to lose only one time, which means there will only be one set of rules of behavior they will have to follow to avoid landing in trouble again in the future. If they were to lose many times, it's possible that the rules of future behavior given to the defendant would be different with each different jury. That would leave defendants confused enough that they might have absolutely no clue what they need to do to avoid making the same mistake twice.

As of 2007, the biggest class action lawsuit ever in America was the case of *Dukes v. Wal-Mart Stores.* The lawsuit began in 2001. Approximately 1.5 million plaintiffs were involved. They demanded Wal-Mart pay them $11 billion to make up for the harm the company caused them. All of the plaintiffs were women who worked at Wal-Mart as far back as 1998. They claimed that they were denied pay raises, job promotions, and better work assignments simply because they were women. They said Wal-Mart violated the Civil Rights Act of 1964 by discriminating against them in this way. Wal-Mart denied doing any such thing. In its defense, the company said it has a long record of championing the needs and interests of its women employees.

Above: Betty Dukes, (right) was the lead plaintiff in a class action lawsuit against Wal-Mart Stores. In the lawsuit, she and 1.5 million plaintiffs claimed that Wal-Mart discriminated against female employees.

Civil Court Rules

Civil courts in America operate using rules that trace back to long before the country was born. Those rules began in England, which had two separate types of courts for handling disputes between people or organizations. One court existed for lawsuits in which money was being demanded to make up for a financial loss brought on by a person's wrongdoing. Perhaps the wrongdoer failed to live up to a contract he had with someone. That would be grounds for a lawsuit seeking payment of what lawyers refer to as *economic damages*. Or perhaps the wrongdoer accidentally crashed his horse-drawn carriage into the carriage of another and caused that person to sprain his back. The owner of the damaged carriage could sue for the money it cost to repair his vehicle in addition to the cost of having his injured back treated. The court might even order the wrongdoer to pay for lost wages while the injured carriage owner recovered from his wounds.

A second English court existed for lawsuits in which the plaintiff wanted a court order to force the defendant to perform a desired task or to stop doing some harmful deed. This was known as seeking an *injunction*. As an example, you might own a nice meadow just outside of town. On the other side of your meadow is a popular beach. There are two ways the people from town can get to the beach. One is the public road that goes the long way around your meadow and takes an hour to travel. The other is straight through the middle of your meadow along a path that takes five minutes to travel. Out of respect for you and your property, everyone from town who goes to the beach takes the public road. Except for one wrongdoer who prefers the path through your meadow. You've caught him several times and have each time politely asked him to get off your land. But he never does. He keeps cutting through your meadow. Finally, you've had enough. So you go to court to do what is called *obtaining relief*.

The judge agrees that the trespassing needs to stop. He then issues an injunction against the wrongdoer. From that time on, the wrongdoer will face fines and maybe even imprisonment if he trespasses again in defiance of the injunction.

Modern American civil courts still give awards of money to people who suffer economic damages, and they continue to issue injunctions on behalf of those who seek to obtain relief. But these different kinds of cases are not handled by different types of courts. And the rules the courts follow nowadays are not quite the same as they were when the country was new. Mainly, the rules are a lot simpler, even though there are a lot more of them. For example, it used to be that you had to be very exact in the way you worded the complaint papers you wrote in order to get a lawsuit started. Your case could be thrown out if the wording was even slightly incorrect. Now the wording is less important than whether your complaint has at its heart the right legal ideas.

Above: A "no trespassing" sign warns people to stay off this property. People who ignore these warnings may be taken to court and served with an injunction. From then on, if the trespasser goes on the owner's property, the wrongdoer may face fines or even imprisonment.

Curtis v. Loether

There's no law that says you must exercise your Seventh Amendment right to have a civil lawsuit tried in front of a jury. You can give up that right if you wish. But you can only give it up if the other side in your lawsuit also agrees.

There was a famous case that came before the U.S. Supreme Court in 1974 in which one side of a lawsuit tried to force the other to have the trial without a jury. The case was known as *Curtis v. Loether*.

In 1968, Congress passed a law called the Civil Rights Act. This law made it illegal to discriminate against people because of the color of their skin. Contained in the Civil Rights Act was a rule that said landlords could be sued for money if they refused to rent a home or apartment to someone of a different race or ethnicity for no reason other than being of a different race or ethnicity. That very thing happened to an African American woman by the name of Ms. Curtis. She wanted to rent an apartment. But the white landlord would not rent to her. So she sued to force the landlord to rent to her and to pay her $1,000 in damages.

The landlord believed he would lose if the case was tried in front of a jury. He felt the jury would have sympathy for the woman to whom he refused to rent the apartment. This led him to demand a trial without a jury. He claimed that the Seventh Amendment right to a jury could only be exercised if both sides agreed to it. She wanted a jury, but he didn't. Therefore, he said no jury was required.

The trial judge agreed with the landlord, pointing out that the Civil Rights Act did not specifically say that juries had to be used in settling disputes under this law. Ms. Curtis thought that was wrong. She took her demand for a jury to a higher court.

Above: Within the 1968 Civil Rights Act is a rule that forbids landlords from refusing to rent to people based solely on their race or ethnicity. When this happened to an African American woman, she sued the white landlord. He did not want the case tried in front of a jury because he thought he would lose. She wanted a jury. The Supreme Court ruled that the Seventh Amendment guarantees that if one side of a lawsuit insists, then they have the right to have the case tried in front of a jury.

The court of appeals heard her argument and agreed, declaring that Ms. Curtis did indeed have a Seventh Amendment right to a jury trial. The court also said that only one side in a lawsuit need ask for a jury.

The landlord appealed the decision, taking the case all the way to the U.S. Supreme Court. The High Court told the landlord that the appeals court had been right in its decision. The Seventh Amendment right to a jury does not depend on whether both sides agree to it.

It Only Takes One

SOME PEOPLE WHO end up in civil court fear having their case tried in front of a jury. They fear it because they believe the jury will feel sorry for the other side. It's an understandable fear. Juries that feel sorry for one side in a case often end up deciding in favor of that person or group. That can happen even if the law is against the side for which the jury feels sympathy.

Because of this, a person who fears losing to the side that gets all the sympathy may try to have the case heard by a judge instead of a jury. That's allowed, but only as long as the other side agrees to it. If the other side says no, then the case must be tried by a jury.

In the late 1980s, a labor union that was being sued by one of its members feared losing because of jury sympathy for the member. So the labor union tried to have the case heard without a jury. The member who was suing would not agree to that. In response, the labor union asked the judge presiding over the trial to dismiss the jury on the grounds that the plaintiff had no right to a jury. The labor union claimed this was one of those situations where the Seventh Amendment guarantee to settle disputes in front of a jury did not apply.

Here's how this all came about: In 1982, a truck driver by the name of Mr. Terry was working for a company that had a contract with the Teamsters Union. The company was McLean Trucking Corporation. It was a big company, but it had run into financial trouble. The company thought it could help solve its money problems by being more efficient. One way it tried to do that was by closing several of its smaller shipping terminals and moving their operations into a single giant location. Mr. Terry was based at one of the smaller terminals. When it closed, the company transferred him to the new, giant terminal.

But then the company laid him off. It rehired him after a few weeks. A while later, it laid him off again. Then it rehired him again. This was hurting Mr. Terry financially. The time he spent laid off was time that he was not earning his usual paycheck.

Above: According to the Seventh Amendment, if one side in a civil lawsuit does not want the case to be heard by a jury, but the other side does, then the case *will* be heard by a jury.

Eventually, Mr. Terry complained to his union and asked for help fixing the problem. But the union did not provide the help that Mr. Terry felt he could expect from it. He then sought relief in court. The targets of his lawsuit were the union and the trucking company. The trucking company later was excused from the lawsuit when it went bankrupt.

That left only the union in the face-off with Mr. Terry. The union's lawyers believed they could not convince a jury to take the union's side in the lawsuit. So they tried to prevent a jury from hearing the lawsuit at all. They did this by claiming that Mr. Terry's Seventh Amendment rights did not extend to lawsuits involving what are known as *collective bargaining agreements*. A collective bargaining agreement is a contract between a business and a labor union. It's a contract that covers things like how much money employees will be paid for their work, how and when they can be laid off, and the processes that will be used in handling complaints the workers might have about their bosses or about the working conditions.

The union said that the Seventh Amendment speaks of lawsuits having to be "according to the rules of the common law." The union's lawyers argued that there was no such thing in the common law as collective bargaining agreements in 1791, the year that the Seventh Amendment was ratified.

This was a clever tactic by the union, but the judge didn't agree with the argument. The union then appealed the judge's decision. The appeal went all the way to the United States Supreme Court. In 1990, the High Court ruled in the case of *Chauffeurs, Teamsters, and Helpers Local Number 391 v. Terry* that the Seventh Amendment does in fact apply to the common law of today, not just the common law of 200 years earlier. The Court pointed out that the common law of today is very aware of collective bargaining agreements. As a result, Mr. Terry could exercise his Seventh Amendment right to have the dispute tried in front of a jury.

Above: Many truckers are members of unions, which use collective bargaining agreements to determine pay and working conditions. In the 1990 case of *Chauffeurs, Teamsters, and Helpers Local Number 391 v. Terry*, the Supreme Court ruled that people may still exercise their right to have a dispute tried in front of a jury, even if there is a collective bargaining agreement not to go to court.

CAN THE GOVERNMENT BE SUED?

Sometimes wrongdoing is committed by the government. For example, say that the government has hired you to mow lawns in your neighborhood this summer. The government promises to pay you $1,000 for every lawn you mow. You get started in June. You finish in August. In that time, you've mowed 500 lawns. You then give the government a bill asking for payment of half a million dollars. But the government decides it's not going to pay you that much. It decides the money is needed for something else. So the government offers to pay you a grand total of $75 for all the lawns you mowed during the summer. In fact, the government doesn't even offer. It just goes ahead and sends you a check for the $75 with a note attached that says take it or leave it.

Lawyers refer to this sort of thing as a *breach of contract*. It's one of the various forms of civil wrongdoing for which the government can be sued. However, there are many, many situations where the government cannot be sued at all. Go back to our example of being hired by the government to mow lawns. This time let's say the government pays you the half a million dollars it owes. But then you add up what you were forced to spend in order to be able to do that job for the government. There was the cost of buying a lawn mower and keeping it in proper working order. There was the cost of transporting the lawn mower around the neighborhood. There was the cost of getting rid of all the grass clippings. There was the cost of sunglasses, sunscreen, cool-looking hat, Bermuda shorts, energy drinks, ice cubes, and all the other items needed to keep you comfortable while you worked.

Above: If you've been asked to do a job at a certain rate of pay, but the employer decides not to pay that amount, it is called a breach of contract.

Most significantly there were the costs of the many items the government required you to have that you didn't realize you needed. They included bright orange safety vests, official lawn-mowing permit, lawn mower operating certificate, grass clippings environmental impact statement, lawn mowing procedures training, liability insurance, and much more. In fact, the things the government required ended up being 90 percent of your total costs. You're horrified to discover that subtracting what you spent from what you earned leaves you owing $75. You can claim you had no idea the government's required items were going to cost so much. You can claim it was unfair of the government to not warn you about these before you agreed to take the job. No matter—you're not allowed to sue.

The reason you're not allowed to sue is that the government has what's known as *sovereign immunity*. That means the government can only be sued if it agrees to let you sue it. This comes from the very old idea that nothing the rulers of a country say or do can ever really be against the law because the rulers are themselves the law in human form.

Such an idea might be fine in a country ruled by a monarch or a dictator. But it doesn't fit very well in the United States, where no one is supposed to be above the law. For that reason, Congress in 1946 passed a law that limited the government's claims to sovereign immunity. Since that time, it has been possible in some situations to sue the government for the wrongdoing of individual government employees without first having to ask the government's permission.

Why would anybody want to sue the government, with or without permission? There are many reasons. For example, there are people who may think the government is not doing enough to catch polluters, or is denying too many basic services to the poor. Then there are people who think the exact opposite. They believe government is doing *too much* to clean up the environment or help the disadvantaged. Taxpayers in particular are often up in arms about what they feel is wasteful government spending.

Generally, though, taxpayers cannot sue the government when they become angry about spending. There is one exception, however. The Supreme Court has ruled it is OK for taxpayers to sue if the spending directly benefits a religion. Such spending is considered unconstitutional because it violates the First Amendment's "establishment of religion" clause.

Above: J.C. Conley stands in front of a map of his hometown of Ketchikan, Alaska, at a committee meeting at the Alaska State Capitol building in Juneau. In 2004, the proposed bridge from Ketchikan (population 7,400) to the city's airport on nearby Gravina Island (population 50) became known as the $328 million "bridge to nowhere." Although government representatives and residents felt it would add to the development of the area, most people were angry at this symbol of wasteful government spending. However, even though they are angry, taxpayers generally cannot sue the United States because the government is protected by sovereign immunity.

They Didn't Sign Away Their Right to Sue

SUSAN AND RICHARD HALLOCK were shocked when they opened the front door of their Mohawk, New York, home and found themselves face to face with federal law-enforcement agents. The agents had a search warrant. They presented it to the Hallocks and entered the home.

The agents were looking for child pornography. They learned that the illegal materials had been purchased online with a credit card belonging to Mr. Hallock. The Hallocks were sure there must have been some mistake. But the agents would not listen, and continued their search.

The agents believed the child pornography was stored on one of the Hallocks' nine computers. The agents logged into them all, one by one. In the end, they found nothing. But they remained convinced the forbidden pornography was stored on at least one of those computers. Possibly it was buried inside a hidden or encrypted file deep within the system. The only way they could be sure was to have the computers examined in a crime lab. There, experts would be able to hack right down to the very bottom of each disk drive.

The agents rounded up the nine computers and carted them off. Months later, the Hallocks received a call from the agents, who said there was absolutely no pornography on any of the computers. They said that what had actually happened was thieves had obtained Mr. Hallock's personal information and used it to apply for credit cards in his name. The thieves then used one of those stolen credit cards to purchase the pornography. The agents thought Mr. Hallock was the one who downloaded the illegal materials because the purchase was made with a credit card under his name.

Left: Police take computer equipment that was believed to have been used for illegal purposes.

Above: The U.S. Capitol in Washington, D.C. While generally protected from lawsuits, the United States government may be sued if its actions are reckless or negligent.

The agents then said they would be returning the computers. When the agents brought them back, they handed the Hallocks a form and told them to sign it. The Hallocks wanted first to know what the form was about. It was a waiver that said the Hallocks agreed not to sue the agents or the government for any damage that might have been done to the computers while the computers were in the custody of the agents.

The Hallocks became immediately suspicious about this and refused to sign the form. Then they turned on the computers. They discovered that the disk drives inside four of them were completely destroyed, and those in a couple of others were badly damaged. The Hallocks used those computers in their home-based software business. The ruined computers contained not only names and account information for all their customers, but also the important formulas used to create the software they sold for a living. Because the computers were damaged, the Hallocks' business was wiped out.

Below: A signed waiver generally means that a person has voluntarily given up their rights.

Since they did not sign the form the agents gave them, the Hallocks could sue for damages. In situations such as this, the government generally cannot claim immunity from lawsuits. The government usually must go to court and defend itself when its employees cause harm through reckless or negligent actions.

An Important Right

The Seventh Amendment does not receive mention very often in the news, unlike the First, Fourth, or Fifth Amendments. Those seem to be in the news almost every day.

But in truth the Seventh Amendment *is* in the news almost every day. Maybe you don't hear about a court case where someone is claiming his or her Seventh Amendment rights were trampled. But you do hear all the time about civil court cases that are tried in front of juries.

Each and every one of those trials is a tribute to the Seventh Amendment. It is because of the Seventh Amendment that government must allow the American people to exercise their right to have personal and business disputes heard in court and to let a jury settle all such matters.

This is a right the people have, but not because government grants it. According to the Constitution, it is a right the people have because they were born with it. The job of the government is to make sure the people's natural-born rights are protected at all times. In the United States, there are an estimated 15 million civil lawsuits threatened or actually filed each year at the federal, state, county, and city level. With numbers like that, it's safe to say the government is doing a very good job of protecting the rights of the people under the Seventh Amendment.

Above: A lawyer argues a case in front of a jury. The United States government must allow the American people to exercise their right to have civil cases, which include personal and business disputes, heard in court and to let juries settle all such matters, if it is so desired by even one of the parties involved.

GLOSSARY

Amendment

When it was created, the Constitution wasn't perfect. The Founding Fathers wisely added a special section. It allowed the Constitution to be changed by future generations. This makes the Constitution flexible. It is able to bend to the will of the people it governs. Changes to the Constitution are called amendments. The first 10 amendments are called the Bill of Rights. An amendment must be approved by two-thirds of both houses of Congress. Once that happens, the amendment must be approved by three-fourths of the states. Then it becomes law. This is a very difficult thing to do. The framers of the Constitution didn't want it changed unless there was a good reason. There have been over 9,000 amendments proposed. Only 27 of them have been ratified, or made into law. Some amendments changed the way our government works. The Twelfth Amendment changed the way we elect our president. The Twenty-Second Amendment limits a president to two terms in office. Constitutional amendments have also increased the freedoms of our citizens. The Thirteenth Amendment finally got rid of slavery. And the Nineteenth Amendment gave women the right to vote.

Bill of Rights

The first 10 amendments to the United States Constitution make up what is known as the Bill of Rights. The Bill of Rights lists the special freedoms every human is born with and is able to enjoy in America. Also, the Bill of Rights tells the government that it cannot stop people from fully using and enjoying those freedoms unless the government has an extremely good reason for doing so.

Defendant

A person, business, or government entity (such as a corporation or town) accused of doing something wrong. In a jury trial, defendants try to defend themselves against the charge or charges placed against them.

Founding Fathers

The men who participated in the Constitutional Convention in 1787, especially the ones who signed the Constitution. Some of the Founding Fathers included George Washington, Benjamin Franklin, John Rutledge, Gouverneur Morris, Alexander Hamilton, and James Madison.

High Court

Another name for the United States Supreme Court.

Jury

A group of ordinary people from all walks of life who make decisions based on evidence presented to them. There are two types of juries. A *petit* jury usually consists of between 9 and 12 people who meet in a courtroom to decide on the guilt or innocence of individuals accused of a crime. Petit juries are usually the kind seen in courtroom dramas on TV or in the movies. Another type of jury is the *grand* jury. This is a group of 12 to 23 people. A grand jury decides whether there is enough evidence against a suspected lawbreaker to have a court trial. The importance of grand juries is that they help make sure prosecutors act honestly and fairly when building a case against someone they accuse of the most serious types of crimes. This helps protect against out-of-control prosecutors trying to send innocent people to prison.

Lawsuit

A legal way to settle a dispute in which both sides argue their case in front of a judge or jury in a court of law. The person who has been wronged is called the plaintiff. The person being sued is called the defendant. Plaintiffs and defendants can be individuals, or they can be businesses or government entities, such as corporations or towns. People can even sue the United States, which is how some cases are filed involving the Constitution and violation of rights.

Sue

To bring a lawsuit against a person or institution in a court of law.

Supreme Court

The United States Supreme Court is the highest court in the country. There are nine judges on the Supreme Court. They make sure local, state, and federal governments are following the rules spelled out in the United States Constitution. Our understanding of the Constitution evolves over time. It is up to the Supreme Court to decide how the Constitution is applied to today's society. When the Supreme Court rules on a case, other courts in the country must follow the decision in similar situations. In this way, the laws of the Constitution are applied equally to all Americans.

Verdict

A judge or jury's decision as to whether a defendant is guilty or innocent in a court trial. The judge or jury comes to this decision after reviewing all the facts of a case made by the defendant and the prosecution.

Witness

A person who swears under oath to tell the truth about something they've seen, heard, or experienced.

INDEX

The U.S. Supreme Court building in Washington, D.C.